THE VALUE OF THE ELEMENTS

Understanding WHY God Brings Us To Specific Places & Experiences

By David Mayorga

Edited by Emily Rose King
©David Mayorga - January 2018

Published by

www.shabarpublications.com

Contents

Foreword	iv
Preface	vi
Chapter 1: The Element of Choice *It Was God Who Made the Two Trees*	1
Chapter 2: The Element of Wicked Leaders *Who Does Pharaoh Think He is?*	7
Chapter 3: The Element of Impossibilities *Why the Red Sea and Why this Way?*	13
Chapter 4: The Element of Deserts *The Emotion of Having Nothing!*	20
Chapter 5: The Element of Giants in Life *Oh! My God, there are Giants in the Land!*	26
Chapter 6: The Element of Losing People in Life *"...my husband is dead..."*	32

Chapter 7: The Element of Surrendering
    The Sound of a Voice Crying Out!   38

Chapter 8: The Element of Pleasing the Father
    Learning to Yield to the Father's Wishes   45

Chapter 9: The Element of Ministry Release
    Why Is the Thief the Treasurer?   50

Chapter 10: The Element of Dying to Self
    Was that Stephen's Last Message?   56

Chapter 11: The Element of Personal Battles
    Paul's Thorn and God's Sufficiency   63

Chapter 12: The Element of Fiery Furnaces
    "Did We Not Cast Three Men Bound Into the Midst of the Fire?"   68

Ministry Resources

Ministry Information

Foreword

When I received a call from a very special friend, colleague, and fellow steward of the revelation of Jesus Christ, I was much honored.

I have known David for more than 40 years. I have seen firsthand his lifelong, relentless pursuit of Christ.

In his latest book The Value of The Elements, his heart has been captured. If you have a profound desire to attain a progressive ever- increasing revelation of Jesus Christ, this book has been written with you in mind.

David has written with such insight about the many elements that Jesus uses to produce conformity to His image in the life of His children.

The admonition for our day has to be what the apostle Paul said, **"Be on the alert, stand firm in the faith, act like men, be strong."** (1 Cor. 16:13) Phillips Modern English translates it, **"live like men."** The Christian church is filled with boys and girls instead of men and women of God.

If you follow the counsel from this godly church leader, you will be on your way to Christian manhood.

David's longtime burden has been to see the children of God set aside all the nonsense that we see in the Christian church today; the nonsense that keeps us and sadly robs us from reaching our highest calling.

There is another David in the Old Testament of whom the Bible says, **"...I have found David the son of Jesse, a man after my heart, who will do all My will."**

(Acts 13:22) The word "will" literally means, "wills."

King David lived a life consumed with this one passion. Some people are content to do the will of God; King David's life was governed by doing all His wills.

By heeding and applying this revelation that has been penned by David Mayorga in this book, you too will be on your way to doing God's wills.

-Gerardo Salmerón, *Senior Pastor of McAllen House of Prayer*

Preface

I heard a man once say, that if a plant desires to grow and be fruitful, it must not rebel against, criticize, or shun away the elements. The elements are vital to its growth process and fruitfulness.

Now, the elements are the dirt, the rain, the sun, and the wind. If we keep that little plant from ever receiving any of these elements, that plant won't grow to its fullest and much less bare fruit.

In today's "microwave" society, many individuals won't put up with the idea that they have to go through any extended process that will bring increase to their lives.

In the secular realm, people won't put up with some form of training, seminar, or schooling to get a promotion at their job, not to mention a higher salary and a better opportunity at life.

In the church life, believers today won't spend a few dollars to attend some valuable training to get a better grasp on God's wisdom to help their desperate situation, or even attend the free of charge early morning prayer meeting to meet God for some desperate repair of brokenness, and position themselves to receive downloads of heavenly revelation.

I firmly believe that the increase that God has prepared for us comes in the elements that He first creates and then brings us into. The elements are so valuable that once we understand what they are and how they work, our lives will bloom amazingly.

While spending some quality time in His presence and very much in the Spirit of the Lord, I brought before the Lord a family who was in dire need, and needed God's consolation, for they had lost a child.

In my desperate crying out to the Lord, His Spirit visited me.

I began to inquire of the Lord regarding the situation at hand and here is what the Holy Spirit said to me, "David, who do you think made or created Pharaoh?" I said, "You Lord."

The Holy Spirit proceeded to educate me on the many different elements God uses to create in us a finer and more focused perspective and vision of how He trains and equips His children. God will use the elements He created, and will then use them to transform us into His image.

It is from this revelation God gave me that glorious morning, that this book was birthed. May it enrich you even more in Him.

-David Mayorga, *Director of Masterbuilder Ministries*

1

THE ELEMENT OF CHOICE
It Was God Who Made the Two Trees

"And the Lord God commanded the man, saying, 'Of every tree of the garden you may freely eat; but of the tree of the knowledge of good and evil you shall not eat, for in the day that you eat of it you shall surely die.'" (Genesis 2:16, 17)

While studying this portion of Scripture, I recognized how simple it is to please the Lord, if one truly desires to do so. Often, believers tend to fail in their attempt to please God and feel guilty and ashamed.

What is more surprising to me is the reaction to failure. Most people don't own up or take responsibility for what choices they have made and begin to blame others for it!

And Indeed It Was Very Good!

In this beginning chapter, I would like to challenge your creativity and take you back into the Garden of Eden.

When God was finished with the creation of man, the Bible says, **"Then God saw everything that He had made, and indeed it was very good."**

From God's perspective, everything He had created was in its perfect place, just the way He envisioned it to be. Every day had its purpose; every day had its design.

Everything God had made was to serve Him and bring glory to Him, including the serpent in Chapter 3 of Genesis.

It is amazing to me how so often people will take the good things God has created, but will not accept the fact that God also created the serpent to serve Him as well.

It Is Not About the Serpent!

As God had completed His task of creating everything that was in His heart, He proceeded to speak with man. In His conversation with him, He said that everything was set in motion and all man had to do was to be responsible with the authority God had given Him.

The Word says, **"Then the Lord God took the man and put him in the garden of Eden to tend and keep it. And the Lord God commanded the man, saying, 'Of every tree of the garden you may freely eat; but of the tree of the knowledge of good and evil you shall not eat, for in the day that you eat of it you shall surely die.'"** (Genesis 2:15-17)

One thing I noticed as I pondered God's words was that He never spoke of the possibility of a serpent hanging out in the Garden of Eden. I would imagine that if the serpent would play such a big role in human history, surely, God would have brought it up in His instruction to Adam.

Maybe God would have said something like, "Hey Adam, as you go about your business of tending the garden, please know that there is a serpent that tends to seduce people with its ability to speak and is very good at convincing people to be rebellious towards Me. Please be on the lookout for it, and be sure you don't fall into all the lies it will say to you."

But here is what I believe God was thinking as He instructed Adam.

God had put his trust in man. All He had to do was tell him that there would be two trees in the garden: one was good for food, and the other tree was not!

Knowing God's Desires

Here is what I believe God was thinking: The Lord was probably thinking that man, though created by Him, would obey Him and trust Him with the instruction.

The instruction was clear: Eat from this tree; don't eat from this other tree. One brings life, and the other brings death!

Knowing the desires of the Lord will help us know which way to go in life. There are so many things we can do and choices we can make as we navigate through life, yet God expects us to make the right choice—the choice that brings joy to His heart.

The Trees Were the Element

In following God's wisdom, one must know that that the element in this story was not the serpent, but rather the trees. God never even mentioned the serpent, not even once.

He did mention the trees in the garden and the possibilities of each. He also mentioned that one of the trees was good for food, while the other would eventually kill them if its fruit was eaten.

You and I will forever deal with the element of the two trees as we live out our lives here on earth.

The temptation will always be the choice, not the serpent. Though the serpent (the devil) appears at different points throughout our lives, it is not the serpent's voice that will make us or break us, but our knowledge of Him, our relationship with God, our burning desire to please the Father—this is what will keep us on the path of righteousness, blessing, and honor.

Stop Blaming the Element

As I minister in His Name throughout our region, I continually encounter some who will come to me and say (with a blaming tone) how this individual or that individual was the cause of their miserable life.

They will start blaming the devil, family members, friends, husbands, wives, jobs, neighbors, the boss at work, even the pastor at their local church, for how their lives have ended up.

I can imagine Adam going off on God and saying, "Why did you play a trick on us? Why did you put two trees in the Garden? Why would you do such a wicked thing like that?"

God would have probably responded: "I created you to love Me and gave you the ability to know Me. I made you in My image with all the power to choose Me, but you chose yourself over Me!"

Man chose to willingly and deliberately disobey God's orders! It's not God's fault, but man's for the chaos in his own life. It is truly man who brings his own pain upon himself.

The Element Is for Man's Benefit

As we learn that the trees were the element to make a man either a failure by the choice he makes, or a son of God by obeying, we must realize that if the right God-choice is made, a greater intimacy will come forth from it.

Every time we keep God's words, we reinforce our relationship with God; our trust in Him grows, our decisions to follow Him closer grow, and our devotion to His will and to His ways increase.

You and I will be tested by the element of choice every single day of our lives here on earth. We will choose to eat of the fruit of life, or we will take a bite of the fruit of the tree of the knowledge of good and evil, which is the tree of self.

The results will eventually manifest themselves in time and our lives will bear the fruit of it. What a man sows into his own garden, that is the fruit he will be eating.

Know God's Perspective

As I close this one point, please realize that before you start blaming the serpent in the garden, first ponder the facts.

It was God who talked to man about two trees in the garden, and never mentioned the serpent.

It was God who expected man to honor His words, not the serpent's words.

The element of choice will forever be part of our earthly lives; so, to keep ourselves within what God wants and desires from us— let us seek God for wisdom.

In seeking His wisdom, we will always know what to do, how to do it, and when to do it.

2

THE ELEMENT OF UNGODLY LEADERS
Who Does Pharaoh Think He Is?

"Then the Lord said to Moses, 'Rise early in the morning and stand before Pharaoh, and say to him, "Thus says the Lord God of the Hebrews: Let My people go, that they may serve Me, for at this time I will send all My plagues to your very heart, and on your servants and on your people, that you may know that there is none like Me in all the earth. Now if I had stretched out My hand and struck you and your people with pestilence, then you would have been cut off from the earth. But indeed for this purpose I have raised you up, that I may show My power in you, and that My name may be declared in all the earth. As yet you exalt yourself against My people in that you will not let them go."'"
(Exodus 9:13-17)

Have you ever read this portion of Scripture and considered it with your heart and mind? It is profound! There are many questions I have regarding the "why" would God raise an ungodly leader to hold back the flow of His purpose on the earth.

You probably have seen it in movies, how God used Pharaoh to hinder the Hebrew children from coming into the wilderness to worship Jehovah God.

Several times, the attempt was made; through plagues and warnings, Pharaoh was commanded to release God's children so they could worship along with their animals and people—but Pharaoh would not let them go!

Who Does Pharaoh Think He is?

Pharaoh was the highest authority in the land during the time of Moses, and anyone under the Pharaoh's jurisdiction had to submit to his leadership.

The Hebrew children were brought into Egypt back when Joseph found favor with the Pharaoh during God's favor upon them. As a new Pharaoh took command, he was not familiar with all the mercy God had shown His children. Listen to this: **"Now there arose a new king over Egypt, who did not know Joseph. And he said to his people, 'Look, the people of the children of Israel are more and mightier than we; come, let us deal shrewdly with them, lest they multiply, and it happen, in the event of war, that they also join our enemies and fight against us, and so go up out of the land.'"** (Exodus 1:8-10)

Obviously, God knew that a new king (Pharaoh) had risen to leadership, and that His children would be facing horrible opposition and end up as slaves.

Here is one thing we need to understand about our loving God: He is never taken by surprise when we face adversity. I would even dare say that God has prepared daily provisions for every occasion that we will ever face in this life.

Let us look a little deeper into the verse in Exodus chapter 9 where it says, **"But indeed for this purpose I have raised you up, that I may show My power in you, and that My name may be declared in all the earth."**

Without doubt and without confusing the matter at hand, God raised up Pharaoh for His good pleasure!

Pharaoh was not in control of anything—Jehovah God was! Too often, believers tend to get all "hyped up" about spiritual warfare and start casting out demons from anything and everything that is negative. They start seeing demons hiding behind every bush or light pole.

Where did this vain idea or philosophy come from that everything negative comes from Satan? Where was it birthed? Was it not birthed in the flesh?

I believe this idea that Satan is making the attempt to destroy God's people was created in someone's carnal mind. I do believe Satan hates God's people and yes, he would destroy them if he could, but he can't! Dying to self is the key to a victorious life.

Believers who have not been to the cross of Christ, those who have never been to Calvary, don't understand the power of dying to self!

Here is the fact: Can a dead man feel anything? The answer is a resounding NO!!! Not even the devil can wake him or her up! So, rest in the death and the resurrection power of Christ in you! When the devil comes knocking at your door—just send Jesus to open it.

Always remember that Pharaoh was God's element to train His people in so many ways. God used this man to teach the Hebrew children to believe and trust in Jehovah God and to lean on Him for everything.

Why Did that Ungodly Leader Come into My Life?

Now, you might be experiencing some difficulty with an ungodly leader. That person might be a family member, your parents (who are not born-again,) a boss at work, a teacher at school, or a harsh leader at church.

Typically, if things are going great, we tend to be happy and joyful with our lot in life. If things are negative, we tend to want to look at whom the culprit is who has made us feel this way.

We quickly turn our attention at the words that were said, or the look that they gave us and conclude, "They are against me."

I have often heard believers say, "My boss at work is the devil! They treat me so unfair; they are so sarcastic and mean to me!"

If we continue looking at people as culprits and don't acknowledge seeing the mighty hand of God upon our situation— we will experience so many "attacks."

When God desires to do something deep in us, He will raise up the "Pharaohs" in our lives. It might be one, two, or three, and sometimes they will all gang up on us.

When Is "the Pharaoh" Leaving Us Alone?

Due to the lack of knowledge and understanding in the things of God, too often the element of ungodly leaders is misinterpreted.

If after rebuking devils, damning people, and bartering with the Lord, things remain the same, we must search for the truth.

Listen my friend, the Pharaoh isn't leaving us alone until the lesson has been reached, learned, and applied.

The element of ungodly leaders was not created so we could practice our authority in Christ; this element was given so we could learn how God uses things—circumstance and people for His glory.

My job as a believer in Christ is to trust Him with every circumstance in my life. I am responsible for getting a hold of the Lord, hearing His voice, applying His principles, and continuing to abide in His presence!

It is not my duty to figure out what demon came my way to attack me, nor what is his name or his address.

God brings elements into my life that have been designed in such a way that it will break me, mold me, reshape me, and fill me with His greater purpose for my life.

When Pharaohs appear before us, we should immediately run to the Lord for covering. We are at our best when we are hidden in Christ in God.

As I close this chapter on the Element of Ungodly Leaders, you must recognize that God is at work in you, and that He will never leave you to fight alone against any Pharaoh in your life.

If there is any piece of wisdom I want to share with you on this, it is found in Psalm 91:

"He who dwells in the secret place of the Most High shall abide under the shadow of the Almighty.

The Value of the Elements

I will say of the Lord, 'He is my refuge and my fortress; My God, in Him I will trust.'
Surely He shall deliver you from the snare of the fowler and from the perilous pestilence.
He shall cover you with His feathers,
And under His wings you shall take refuge;
His truth shall be your shield and buckler.
You shall not be afraid of the terror by night,
Nor of the arrow that flies by day,
Nor of the pestilence that walks in darkness,
Nor of the destruction that lays waste at noon day.
A thousand may fall at your side,
And ten thousand at your right hand;
But it shall not come near you.
Only with your eyes shall you look,
And see the reward of the wicked."
(Psalm 91:1-8)

3

THE ELEMENT OF IMPOSSIBILITIES
Why the Red Sea and Why this Way?

"Then it came to pass, when Pharaoh had let the people go, that God did not lead them by way of the land of the Philistines, although that was near; for God said, 'Lest perhaps the people change their minds when they see war, and return to Egypt.' So God led the people around by way of the wilderness of the Red Sea. And the children of Israel went up in orderly ranks out of the land of Egypt." (Exodus 13:17-18)

After the people of God had been treated unfairly, they cried out to God, and the Lord answered them by raising up Moses as their deliverer. Moses shows up on the scene with great anointing, doing signs and wonders, and then confronts Pharaoh.

It was God's design that God's people would reach a desperate time in their lives and desire to break free from the bondage of slavery they were under.

I believe that a desire to break free is a desire placed in the human heart by God for the purpose of bringing that vessel into a season of preparation for the sake of purpose.

People often wonder why some stay stuck in the same place all their lives. The answer to that, from my estimation, is due to the lack of maturity in the individual. There is no burning desire to enter into God's purpose for their lives, thus, the stagnation.

Many believers today are content to stay this way. They live on yesterday's manna; they drink from the cisterns of past experiences, and the fact that they are accepted and wanted in their churches and ministries makes it all the more appealing to never move!

God usually stirs the heart of the individual He is getting ready; he does this by stirring his emotions, trying his motives, stretching his faith, etc.

God was getting ready to move His people out from Egypt, and the process of shifting is usually never an easy one.

Being in slavery for some 400 years was no easy thing to overcome. Habits, manners, culture, structure, mindsets, practices, and hard taskmasters were going to be some hurdles that they would have to cross.

For the breaking of these practices and habits, God had a plan, a wise plan. God knew His people's hearts and knew how frail and fickle they were. So God designed a master plan to get them up and going into His purpose.

His Knowledge Makes It Easier

As the Lord brings His vessels to a crossroads in their faith, a testing of their faith, if you will— it is hardly ever a "hop, skip, and a jump." There will be adversity, challenges, and sometimes perhaps casualties.

Those who embrace the elements will always proceed forth as gold. Those who understand the ways of heaven will always know the ways of God.

For some reason, I am reminded of the words of Jesus when He said, **"Come to Me, all you who labor and are heavy laden, and I will give you rest. Take My yoke upon you and learn from Me, for I am gentle and lowly in heart, and you will find rest for your souls. For My yoke is easy and My burden is light."** (Matthew 11:28-30)

Jesus promises rest to as many as come to Him, take His yoke, and learn from Him. He adds, **"...My yoke is easy and My burden is light."** Oh! That we could get a glimpse of this revelation— that it might free us from ourselves!

Once we understand that it is the Father who holds the elements in His hands, we will quickly discover the rest that Jesus speaks of.

As long as we continue to try and figure out the elements all by ourselves, we will go in circles for all eternity. The minute we understand the revelation that it is God, who makes things move around us, over us, under us and in us, then we will have reached the beginning of His wisdom.

God's Motive Revealed of Why through the Red Sea

If you read the passage in Exodus 13:17-18, you will notice the wisdom of God revealed. In this verse, you will find out the real reason why God took the Hebrew children through the Red Sea, and not around it or some other quick way. As I had stated before, God knew His people and how frail and fickle they were. Based on knowing His own creation in depth, God decided that it would be better to take them through the Red Sea, rather than around it.

Listen to the words God was speaking in regards to His own children, **"Lest perhaps the people change their minds when they see war, and return to Egypt."**

What God was really saying here was that His own people would face war, and they would change their minds about the Promised Land. They would more than likely decide to leave the promise God made them due to the fear in their own minds. They would totally abort the plan of God and return to old Egypt.

So, God in His wisdom, decided that it would be better to take them through the Red Sea and cross it on dry ground and in this way, they would have no way of coming back to Egypt. God knows all our selfish tendencies.

The Element of the Red Sea

When the children of Israel reached the Red Sea, they noticed that there was no more room to go forward. So they wondered and wondered, then they panicked!

What do you say to yourself when you see an obstacle? Do you see an impossibility? Do you see a possibility for God to do something of wonder? What is your mindset towards the Red Seas in your own life? This is the very thing that plagued the Hebrew children.

Now, let us look at some of the things we find out about God's people as they begin to undergo the most excruciating test to date in the trying of their faith:

"And the Lord hardened the heart of Pharaoh

king of Egypt, and he pursued the children of Israel; and the children of Israel went out with boldness. So the Egyptians pursued them, all the horses and chariots of Pharaoh, his horsemen and his army, and overtook them camping by the sea beside Pi Hahiroth, before Baal Zephon. And when Pharaoh drew near, the children of Israel lifted their eyes, and behold, the Egyptians marched after them. So they were very afraid, and the children of Israel cried out to the Lord. Then they said to Moses, "Because there were no graves in Egypt, have you taken us away to die in the wilderness? Why have you so dealt with us, to bring us up out of Egypt? Is this not the word that we told you in Egypt, saying, 'Let us alone that we may serve the Egyptians'? For it would have been better for us to serve the Egyptians than that we should die in the wilderness." And Moses said to the people, "Do not be afraid. Stand still, and see the salvation of the Lord, which He will accomplish for you today. For the Egyptians whom you see today, you shall see again no more forever. The Lord will fight for you, and you shall hold your peace." And the Lord said to Moses, "Why do you cry to Me? Tell the children of Israel to go forward. But lift up your rod, and stretch out your hand over the sea and divide it. And the children of Israel shall go on dry ground through the midst of the sea." (Exodus 14:8-16)

Did you catch the attitudes that the element (of the Red Sea) brought out of them?

As long as there was no one pursuing them, the

children of Israel were "amen-ing" and praising God, but the minute they found out that Pharaoh was chasing them, they went bonkers! Oh, to know the wisdom of God.

The fear came out, the blaming came out, their indecision came out, etc.

There are so many believers who are just like these Hebrew children: Everything is "happy pills" until the Red Sea blocks them, and now they have to deal with themselves!

The element of the Red Sea was the tool God used to block the children of Israel from advancing into their Promised Land. Only those who would march forward would have a chance to experience the promise.

The Hebrew children were now facing mountains on each side because of the wilderness, the army of Pharaoh coming after them and a Red Sea that wouldn't let them pass.

What can a man do in this situation? What can anyone do facing this desperate situation? What would you do if you were in the Hebrew children's shoes? Would you start climbing the mountains? Would you start fighting Pharaoh's mighty army? Would you start swimming across the Red Sea? Or would you wait upon God's word of instruction? What would you do?

Why Do You Cry to Me, Go Forward!

"And Moses said to the people, "Do not be afraid. Stand still, and see the salvation of the Lord..." Moses' counsel to the children of Israel was for them to not be afraid and to stand still and watch what God would do. This sounds comforting—but was it?

Apparently, these words didn't seem to comfort the fearful Hebrew children until God broke through with revelatory knowledge. Listen to this: "And the Lord said to Moses, "Why do you cry to Me? **Tell the children of Israel to go forward. But lift up your rod, and stretch out your hand over the sea and divide it. And the children of Israel shall go on dry ground through the midst of the sea.**"

Moses had a great understanding of the power of God, but God's people were stuck or better yet, they were paralyzed by fear. Nothing moves a paralyzed individual like a miracle, and nothing could move God's paralyzed Hebrew children but a heavenly word saying, "Why do you cry to Me? Go forward!"

It wasn't until God revealed to Moses what He needed done, that the people advanced forward on dry ground.

The element of impossibilities will follow all who believe. We will all be challenged at one time or another to cross our own impossibilities.

More than a decoration on the planet, and a sea to house fish, the Red Sea was a tool in God's hands. It was to be an element that would reveal the true nature of His own children as they endeavored to enter into their promise. So, it will be with you and I.

4

THE ELEMENT OF DESERTS
The Emotion of Having Nothing!

"**Every commandment which I command you today you must be careful to observe, that you may live and multiply, and go in and possess the land of which the Lord swore to your fathers. And you shall remember that the Lord your God led you all the way these forty years in the wilderness, to humble you and test you, to know what was in your heart, whether you would keep His commandments or not. So He humbled you, allowed you to hunger, and fed you with manna, which you did not know nor did your fathers know, that He might make you know that man shall not live by bread alone; but man lives by every word that proceeds from the mouth of the Lord. Your garments did not wear out on you, nor did your foot swell these forty years. You should know in your heart that as a man chastens his son, so the Lord your God chastens you.**" (Deuteronomy 8:1-5)

When we hear the word desert, immediately a negative emotion overcomes us, and to be honest, it is not a place that we long for.

A desert is usually not that wonderful place where you vacation and go parasailing or scuba diving, or much less lay out in the nice 78-degree weather on a chair by a pool. No sir! Not in a desert.

As a matter of fact, the desert is probably the direct opposite of where anyone would desire to go for a vacation; it is a place that is usually extremely hot, arid, and very lonely.

Deserts have been known to symbolize those places in life or those seasons in life we all face when everything seems to be dry and lonely. Have you ever been to the desert? That place where you feel nothing, you are going nowhere, and as far as you are concerned, giving up would be the right thing to do while you still have breath in you.

I believe deserts have very specific purposes in our walk with God and if ignored, we might never get out of it!

The element of deserts is what God uses to test the vessels' heart, devotion, resolve (commitment), and persistence.

God is After Our Hearts

Why would God use a desert-like experience to test the hearts of the Hebrew children as they marched through the desert land? Here's what I got as I studied this one passage: **"And you shall remember that the Lord your God led you all the way these forty years in the wilderness, to humble you and test you, to know what was in your heart, whether you would keep His commandments or not."** (Deuteronomy 8:2)

An important thing to know about deserts is that they do test everything about you, both inward and outward.

Now the Hebrew children were so excited with the initial fact of breaking out of Egypt and following God's leadership through Moses, that it seemed like an excellent idea, and they were determined to follow through no matter what!

Most believers tend to be this way when they get exuberantly emotional with opportunities to do something or go somewhere that involves the Lord. Yet, when the actual "walk" starts, they begin to complain and whine of how it is so hard, and they may even comment on how maybe they should have stayed behind and not have made the trip. Have you heard this? Have you done this yourself?

The Typical Cry from the Immature

I have watched this course of action, attitude, or expression come forth from believers throughout my time serving Jesus and it is so consistent with Bible patterns.

What exactly am I making specific reference to? I am making a specific reference to the type of response immature believers have when they are invited to go on a mission's trip, when they are called upon to lead a new ministry, when they are called to be the person in charge of a certain program—they get excited and very humbled by the opportunity. This is all good. But...

When the process begins and one has to grind to "make it happen," they become disconcerted, confused, angry, and quickly find ways to bail out from the opportunity given to them by the Lord. This is all too common.

Without knowledge of what a desert is and what its intention is— the servant of the Lord aborts the work at hand, criticizes the lack of support from others, and shuts down.

God's Intention for the Desert

As we read earlier, the intention of the Lord is really all that matters. When we are tested, it would be wise to recognize what is what the Lord is after. What is the Lord attempting to convey to us?

First, Moses speaks to the children of Israel and says to them: **"And you shall remember that the Lord God led you all the way these forty years in the wilderness..."**

Here is what we need to come to grips with: It was God who led us for forty years in the wilderness. This goes to show, that God was not oblivious, not even for one second, that His children were walking around in a desert for forty years. In other words, God knew about the desert, and God used the desert for His purposes.

Yes, He will do the same for us! We must see the desert with the same eyes and intent that God had.

God was very clear and states a few purposes for the desert experience: 1) to humble you 2) to test you and 3) to know what is in your heart.

Nothing Like the Emotion of Being Humbled

I don't think that there is anything even close to the feeling of being humbled by someone or something. Humility takes us back to our roots. Maybe I should say it this way: Humility takes us back to our original state—dust! God wants us to remember who we are and who is responsible for making us stand.

Humility in its basic form means to me, "God first in everything!" We don't make a move in our own strength, idea, concept and/or intellect. We wait upon the Lord for revelation knowledge, and then we move according to His desire.

A Healthy Heavenly Test

Moses also reminded the children of Israel that they were not only being humbled by the experience, but that they would be tested as well.

Testing is a bad word to so many. Testing to some brings flashbacks of when they were in school and how they had to study and study to pass exams. That explains the countless nightmares.

Now, for some, testing is a good thing. It's a marker of accomplishment and a measure of if one has learned the necessary lessons for the next chapter in life.

Nevertheless, God tested the children of Israel. I'm sure the test had a lot to do with faith, devotion and perhaps perseverance.

What Is Really in Your Heart?

The desert also brought the children of Israel to the harsh reality of what was really in their hearts. God will know our hearts by our response to the element of deserts in our personal life.

How we react and respond to the loneliness, dryness and forsakenness if it all, will tell the story, our story!

Don't Need Fleshly Comfort but a Revelation of Christ!

The element of the desert has a natural way of breaking us down. It begins by removing all the fleshly emotions that are dependent upon more of the same.

No one calls, no one speaks to us, no one seeks us, no one cares about our accomplishments, no one comes to our ministry or bible study, no one comes to our place of business, no one praises you anymore, no one really cares what you do for a living, no one gets excited about your new-found experience with God, no one, no one, no one!

This makes you go deeper and ask deeper questions regarding yourself, God, and your purpose in life. The seeking will drive you to a place of revelation. It will squeeze the honey out of you!

Remember to never discard the many deserts you will experience in your own walk with the Lord. After you have survived the desert, you will be endued with wisdom, fresh revelation, and power!

5

THE ELEMENT OF GIANTS IN LIFE
Oh! My God, there are Giants in the Land!

"Now they departed and came back to Moses and Aaron and all the congregation of the children of Israel in the Wilderness of Paran, at Kadesh; they brought back word to them and to all the congregation, and showed them the fruit of the land. Then they told him, and said: 'We went to the land where you sent us. It truly flows with milk and honey, and this is its fruit. Nevertheless the people who dwell in the land are strong; the cities are fortified and very large; moreover we saw the descendants of Anak there. The Amalekites dwell in the land of the South; the Hittites, the Jebusites, and the Amorites dwell in the mountains; and the Canaanites dwell by the sea and along the banks of the Jordan.'

Then Caleb quieted the people before Moses, and said, 'Let us go up at once and take possession, for we are well able to overcome it.'

But the men who had gone up with him said, 'We are not able to go up against the people, for they are stronger than we.' And they gave the children of Israel a bad report of the land which they had spied out, saying, 'The land through which we have gone as spies is a land that devours its inhabitants, and all the people whom we saw in it are men of great stature. There we saw the giants (the descendants of

Anak came from the giants); and we were like grasshoppers in our own sight, and so we were in their sight.'" (Numbers 13:26-33)

I have often wondered why the Lord will call us to go forward into a new venture and the minute we do, we are confronted with great opposition. Why does this happen?

For some odd reason, God has always been about personal development. It is my conviction that God is more interested in our transformation, than whatever He has in mind to give us. This is the mind of the Lord.

Now, I also know that some are not as in tune with this philosophy as I have been for years, but you will discover as you study the Scriptures, that God is about transformation more than He is about any great accomplishment.

God Knows All Things

As the Lord instructed His people to possess the land, and assured them that if they would march forward they would have it, the people's faith waned. The people started to back-peddle at the instruction of the Lord and chose to send twelve spies instead (just to make sure that what God had promised was true.)

After forty days of researching and studying the land, they saw that what the Lord had told them was real. The fruit was awesome and the land prosperous!

Most of us react with excitement during the initial phase of a new project, and then somehow convince ourselves that we can have it if we try hard enough. Isn't this true about us?

As the children of Israel were scoping out the land and excited about their findings, they came across some people who appeared to be of great stature. As they looked closer, they noticed that these guys were giants!

Keep in mind that God knew this all along. God knew that His people would be confronted with their own weaknesses.

Suddenly the dream that God had painted for them became more and more distant; the giants seem to be getting bigger and bigger, and the possibilities of ever entering into God's promise were left on a shelf.

The Report

The report of the spies was based upon what their eyes saw and what their ears heard, not on what God had spoken. Every test must be apprehended by faith or else we will fail it!

Now, of the twelve spies, ten of them were against the idea of possessing the land, only two of them were for it. Joshua and Caleb were men of a different spirit and had a different set of faculties - they believed God!

Is it any wonder why these two mighty servants of God eventually possessed the land God had promised them? There is a reason why some people possess the land and some don't! There is a real reason why some walk in God's best and others never will.

God's Vision Must Be Done God's Way!

Here is what I typically find in men and women of God who are challenged to pursue the heart of God—

God will reveal His will for them and how they must get to God's desired end, but the servant of God will not follow the voice of God in His endeavor.

God knew exactly what He was doing with His children; He always does!

He knew that His children would probably doubt His plan and vision, yet in His love, He shared it with them. He told them to go and take the land for it was theirs.

So the people of God decided to meet God halfway; they decided to send spies first, then if things were good, they would press onward to cross the Jordan and live happily after.

Here is what happens: God's vision must be done God's way. It is the best way; it is the only way!

The Element will do Three Things

The element will provoke three things to come forth in us, but it is a holy provocation.

First, the element will cause you to see yourself as you really are or who you really are. All the fears, doubts, and abilities or lack there of, will be viciously exposed. It is vital for the element to do this to us. If we don't recognize who we really are, then we will not know how much of God we truly need.

The error in many is the carnal mind. People tend to take a light approach at following God's will, then

The Value of the Elements

quickly realize how much of God they truly need.

Secondly, the element will cause you to see how big the element really is. As the children of Israel keep looking at the giants, they also saw how small they were.

The element has this effect—it makes us look at it so that we might size it up. Once we do, it is a natural tendency to size ourselves up in the presence of said element. It is there when we make our conclusions: We are too small, too insignificant, too weak, too dumb, too stupid, unable and unskilled.

When we compare ourselves with ourselves, it can be a grim reality. That is why we don't do this: We measure ourselves hidden in Christ. **"For you died, and your life is hidden with Christ in God. When Christ who is our life appears, then you also will appear with Him in glory."** (Colossians 3: 3,4: 3,4)

Thirdly, the element will cause us either to run and hide, or it will cause us to look at God in a different way!

So often, we have aborted countless sets of instructions all because we felt we couldn't complete them. We failed to look at God, the Author and Finisher of our faith!

Always remember: If God ever told you to do something for His Name's sake, that along with the promises come the set of instructions. It is truly God's idea and it will make provisions for it all the way through.

He will speak to your heart, and He will guide you through step one and walk with you until His project is completed. Do you believe this?

Every Giant is on a Leash!

Every giant that has appeared in your own life, and every giant that will ever appear in your life is on a leash. Giants are God's tools to do you good. They will not hurt you, but rather they will help you go deeper with God.

The element of giants that appears in your life can only mean one thing: It is the illusion of an obstacle pretending to be bigger than the God whom you serve; that thing that is trying to keep you away from entering into a deeper and wider relationship with God; giants are the epitome of fear and paralysis from your forward motion in God and His promises.

Oh! And by the way, the fruit is pretty awesome too- not to mention the milk and the honey.

6

THE ELEMENT OF LOSING PEOPLE
"...my husband is dead..."

"A certain woman of the wives of the sons of the prophets cried out to Elisha, saying, 'Your servant my husband is dead, and you know that your servant feared the Lord. And the creditor is coming to take my two sons to be his slaves.'

So Elisha said to her, 'What shall I do for you? Tell me, what do you have in the house?' And she said, 'Your maidservant has nothing in the house but a jar of oil.'

Then he said, 'Go, borrow vessels from everywhere, from all your neighbors—empty vessels; do not gather just a few. And when you have come in, you shall shut the door behind you and your sons; then pour it into all those vessels, and set aside the full ones.'

So she went from him and shut the door behind her and her sons, who brought the vessels to her; and she poured it out. Now it came to pass, when the vessels were full, that she said to her son, 'Bring me another vessel.'

And he said to her, 'There is not another vessel.' So the oil ceased. Then she came and told the man of God. And he said, 'Go, sell the oil and pay your debt; and you and your sons live on the rest.'" (2 Kings 4:1-9)

There are so many events that happen in a lifetime, and I believe that one of the greatest but saddest events is when a family member dies or maybe even a close relative or friend.

Coping with a test of this magnitude has to be one of the hardest emotions to deal with.

In this chapter, I want to address the element of losing someone of great value in your life.

As I have ministered in my life for over thirty plus years, I have had the opportunity to conduct many funerals. All funerals are the same but different.

They are the same in that the end-result will pretty much be synonymous, being that one will be laid down to rest, yet they will also be different, in that the level of impact will differ in how much significance the death will have on some members of the family.

Some people will cry more than others, while others will get over the death and burial in a shorter time.

Your Servant My Husband Is Dead!

It came to pass in Israel that this man of God had passed away and apparently, his monetary contribution to his household was huge and after his death no one was able to make the payments to his creditors.

Can you imagine the emotion this widow was experiencing? The loss of her husband, the loss of her belongings, and now the possible loss of her children to the creditors. What a test!

This specific element has a way of making us cry out in despair to a God who is ever mindful of us. It will make us go deeper, pray longer, and make us more determined to receive answers.

One can attempt to make a case against God for allowing this servant of God and sole family breadwinner to die.

Did God know of their needs? Yes! Did God know what they would be facing? Yes! Did God know it would mean that this family would have to establish a new order in their lifestyle? Yes!

God Always Has a Solution

As the Prophet Elisha heard this woman's testimony, he could easily sense her need and despair. Elisha is a type of God in this case; he represents Jehovah in this picture.

We must always acknowledge while being tested, God has His eye upon us. He will not let us deal with our issues alone; He is that faithful.

The picture we get of this widow speaking to Elisha is also the same idea of pleading when we come to God with our own circumstances.

Here are two questions that God wants us to reflect upon:
1) What shall I do for you?
2) What do you have in the house?

As we face the loss of someone or something, the feeling is hard to describe. All kinds of emotions run through our mind and heart. But as you press inward and touch the Lord in prayer, you will discover that God truly is there and is ready to help us with whatever will help us stabilize and move us forward.

In this story, God is saying through Elisha, "What shall I do for you? This is what happens when you stay calm during the storm. One will be able to pray and hear the heart of God and know His concern. All we must do now is ask what we need from Him, be as specific as you can be.

The second question might be in relation to what you can do to better your situation. In this case, Elisha asked the widow, **"What do you have in your house?"** By context, it was obvious that this widow had nothing! Everything she owned had been collected already by the creditors. Why was God (in this case Elisha) asking for anything in the house?

God will often ask us to go deep and search for the answer we need within us. He created us and equipped us with everything we need to make it in this life!

Nothing in the house, but...

The widow says, **"Your maidservant has nothing in the house but a jar of oil."** When the Prophet Elisha heard that, her further instructed her: **"Go, borrow vessels from everywhere, from all your neighbors— empty vessels; do not gather just a few. And when you have come in, you shall shut the door behind you and your sons; then pour it into all those vessels, and set aside the full ones."**

The widow was on to something! God had heard her cry and was now about to turn a hard situation into an opportunity for a miracle. This is so like the Lord to do things like this. He doesn't need much to make a miracle, but He does require human cooperation.

When there were no more vessels to fill, the oil stopped flowing. By this time, God had poured enough oil into her vessels that she could now sell it and have a secure future by profiting from it.

What once appeared as a dead-end situation, God turned around by releasing His wisdom through the Prophet Elisha into the widow's mind and heart. The woman moved with what Elisha had instructed her, and her need was met.

With God, Losing Means Gaining

When I meditate upon this story, I find that loses do come. Things do fall apart for some of us— but God is always near to hear our cry. The Bible is filled with these types of promises.

When the crisis of losing someone or something valuable in our lives hits us, the best path to take is the road of seeking after God. To do the opposite, to run and hide, to isolate oneself from people that care and love you, would be a grave mistake. To blame God and to run

I believe that these things do happen in our lives with the intent to further develop our faith and strengthen our resolve in God.

It would be easy to enter a time of depression and worry and fear. Many do!

This element is particularly valuable because it teaches us believers that if we put our trust in Jesus and allow ourselves to be led by His Holy Spirit, there is no dead-end.

One might think that things have ended, but the truth is that God was just stretching out our faith, and teaching us to put our trust in Him, rather than in things and/or people.

7

THE ELEMENT OF SURRENDERING
The Sound of a Voice Crying Out!

"There was a man sent from God, whose name was John. This man came for a witness, to bear witness of the Light that all through him might believe. He was not that Light, but was sent to bear witness of that Light." (John 1:6-8)

Have you ever peeked into the life of John the Baptist? Have you ever considered his upbringing, his obedience, his sacrifice and finally his beheading for righteousness sake?

Let's dive in into the subject of the value of surrendering and go deeper into this beautiful portrait of brokenness.

A Man Sent from God

There is no mistaking the life and message of John the Baptist. Here we have a man born in due season to come as a forerunner of God's kingdom here on earth. He was called to prepare the way of the Lord and to make God's path straight. He was released to announce the manifestation of the Lamb of God, Jesus Christ. What a ministry!

Now, did John self-propagate himself? No! Was John the Baptism a self-proclaimed prophet or voice for God? No!

The Scriptures clearly say that John was "a man sent from God!"

A Cry in the Wilderness

"**In those days John the Baptist came preaching in the wilderness of Judea, and saying, 'Repent, for the kingdom of heaven is at hand!' For this is he who was spoken of by the prophet Isaiah, saying:**

"**The voice of one crying in the wilderness: 'Prepare the way of the LORD; Make His paths straight.'**"

"**Now John himself was clothed in camel's hair, with a leather belt around his waist; and his food was locusts and wild honey. Then Jerusalem, all Judea, and all the region around the Jordan went out to him and were baptized by him in the Jordan, confessing their sins.**" (John 3:1-6)

The life of John the Baptist didn't begin in his ministry in the wilderness. There were at least thirty some years of preparation that went into this man. Broken for the sake of God's purposes, John the Baptist was led by the Spirit into becoming the "voice" God wanted.

Born Out of Barrenness

"**There was in the days of Herod, the king of Judea, a certain priest named Zacharias, of the division of Abijah. His wife was of the daughters of Aaron, and her name was Elizabeth. And they were both righ-**

teous before God, walking in all the commandments and ordinances of the Lord blameless. But they had no child, because Elizabeth was barren, and they were both well advanced in years." (Luke 15:5-7)

All of God's greatest works and workers have been born out of barrenness. Starting with nothing but a vision from the Lord, these (those born out of barrenness) servants launch into the deep with God and accomplish far greater exploits than those who "naturally" purpose them!

These men are not waiting for the "green light" of man's approval; they are waiting for the "sound of the gun" that comes from the throne of heaven like thunder in their spirits! It is the sound of the Lord that they hear and move purposefully into the midst of the fire, God's fire.

"You Shall Call His Name John"

"But the angel said to him, "Do not be afraid, Zacharias, for your prayer is heard; and your wife Elizabeth will bear you a son, and you shall call his name John. And you will have joy and gladness, and many will rejoice at his birth. For he will be great in the sight of the Lord..." (Luke 1:13-15a)

Zachariah came from a lineage where the custom was to name the firstborn after the father; in this case it would be Zacharias. People are always trying to depend upon what they know, which is an old order of doing things. When God calls you up to meet Him, it is usually to release a "new order" of doing things. As good as the past is— it is what it is, the past! God is forever doing new things.

The Lord specifically tells Zacharias that his child will be called John. This would later challenge the status quo of his day!

Traditions Must Come Down

"So it was, on the eighth day, that they came to circumcise the child; and they would have called him by the name of his father, Zacharias. His mother answered and said, 'No, he shall be called John.' But they said to her, 'There is no one among your relatives who is called by this name.' So they made signs to his father — what he would have him called. And he asked for a writing tablet, and wrote, saying, 'His name is John.' So they all marveled. Immediately his mouth was opened and his tongue loosed, and he spoke, praising God. Then fear came on all who dwelt around them; and all these sayings were discussed throughout all the hill country of Judea. And all those who heard them kept them in their hearts, saying, 'What kind of child will this be?' And the hand of the Lord was with him." (Luke 1:59-66)

In the traditions of the forefathers, everyone was looking for little Zacharias running around in the temple, but it wasn't meant to be that way! God had a plan and a purpose, yes, even if it meant breaking the tradition of naming a firstborn just like the father!

This new move of God was so noticeable that it had people wondering, **"What kind of child will this**

be?" God was well on His way to bring about His purpose upon the earth through this young servant of the Lord.

The value of surrendering is not for the uncommitted and whiny believer. Don't for one minute think that is the easy road to success either.

Understanding the value of surrendering can be one of the greatest keys to unfolding one's future.

Content to be God's Voice

"So the child grew and became strong in spirit, and was in the deserts till the day of his manifestation to Israel." (Luke 1:80)

Now John left to the wilderness to live his life; this was His purpose. God had instilled this in John's spirit.

The Scripture says that, **"...the child grew and became strong in the Spirit, and was in the desert."**

Who says the surrendering is not a valuable thing? Who says you can't become strong in the deserts of testing and loneliness? Who says that you can't grow strong in spirit when you're all alone? John did!

He didn't need brothers or sisters to gather around him and tell him how much he was loved, appreciated and accepted. No sir! The Spirit of the Lord was everything to him.

Now John could have "been somebody." His dad Zacharias, **"was a priest, of the division of Abijah. His wife was of the daughters of Aaron..."** (Luke 1:5) This young man had so many "contacts!" He could have run with the carnal circle of friends and been around some very influential people of his day— but no!

Even when his ministry began to get some "publicity" and began to become recognized by those around, John quickly killed that notion and said, **"He must increase, but I must decrease!"** (John 3:30)

This is what years of brokenness at the hands of the Master will do to you! This is the result of understanding the value of surrendering.

God had touched this young man and God Himself would be handcrafting him. Do you want God to handcraft you? Listen to His voice and quickly obey! Don't become bitter in the process of surrendering.

The Greatest Honor – Serving the King!

"The next day John saw Jesus coming toward him, and said, 'Behold! The Lamb of God who takes away the sin of the world! This is He of whom I said, "After me comes a Man who is preferred before me, for He was before me." I did not know Him; but that He should be revealed to Israel, therefore I came baptizing with water.' And John bore witness, saying, 'I saw the Spirit descending from heaven like a dove, and He remained upon Him. I did not know Him, but He who sent me to baptize with water said to me, "Upon whom you see the Spirit descending, and remaining on Him, this is He who baptizes with the Holy Spirit." And I have seen and testified that this is the Son of God.'" (John 1:29-32)

One of the biggest mysteries I've found in the life

of John the Baptist: Why did John the Baptist's ministry come to a screeching halt after Jesus appeared on the scene? Would it be fair for anyone? Would it be fair to prepare for thirty-some years and the ministry only last two, or at most three years? This is what a life led by the Spirit is! This is truly appreciating the value of surrender.

8

THE ELEMENT OF PLEASING THE FATHER
Learning to Yield to the Father's Wishes

"He went a little farther and fell on His face, and prayed, saying, 'O My Father, if it is possible, let this cup pass from Me; nevertheless, not as I will, but as You will.'" (Matthew 26:39)

One of the characteristics that I have admired in almost every person who has accomplished something impactful in life is the selflessness that accompanies their value system and philosophy of life.

Too often, many who would be great, forfeit their vision, calling, or endeavor, because they can't get over themselves. Nothing hinders forward expression more than when a man who thinks more highly than what he ought to.

Jesus Christ, our Lord and King was a man filled with humility, and brokenness. A man who would not dare overstep, usurp, or go against the Father's wishes.

It is important to know this about the man Christ Jesus, (our example) before we dive into our subject matter in this chapter. Christ knew who the Father was; Christ knew who He was and what He had been sent to do.

Making a Godly Choice

In our text above, we find Jesus with three of His disciples during an hour of prayer.

The disciples were good followers, but did not have the heart of God in them. They only followed externally; they only did what they were told to do by Jesus.

The hour of pain had finally arrived in the life of Jesus and some major decisions had to be made. The main decision at hand was to choose death on a cross, or walk away from it.

On one hand, Jesus didn't owe anything to anyone; He could have said, "Have a good life humanity!" and gone back to the glory He had before He came to earth.

The other choice was to carry His cross all the way to Calvary's cross and die the horrible humiliating death of a criminal, for the sake of the sins of the world.

His body was so stressed and overcome with the burden that the Scripture says, **"And being in anguish, he prayed more earnestly, and his sweat was like drops of blood falling to the ground."** (Luke 22:44).
Can you imagine the pressure of the situation He was under?

This is what we call the element of pleasing the Father; when you have the choice to serve yourself, but you choose instead to follow the Father's heart rather than save your own life. Powerful principle!

It's Either God or Me?

When it comes down to pleasing our heavenly Father, it is for His good pleasure. He doesn't force us to do anything. He doesn't push us to take His side, but waits for us to acknowledge our need to obey our Father.

The more alive we are to ourselves, the harder it is to let go of our selfish ambitions, plans, goals and vision. The more "dead" we are to ourselves, the easier it is to embrace His purpose for us.

Walking with Jesus is not as easy as people make it sound. It takes tremendous sacrifice of self so Christ can live and move in us.

The element of pleasing the Father will come to us for God knows if anything else has our hearts or not.

The Father/Son Relationship Tilts the Balance

If there is a relationship between the Father and you, then you will be able to relate better to Him and what plans He has for you. If your relationship with the Father is not too close, very distant, or even broken, you will struggle to discern what He wants from you.

Prayer is one of the best spiritual exercises to develop this intimacy with the Father; it is the greatest tool to make a hard-hearted man come to his senses in the area of humility. Prayer will bring anyone into direct contact with God's heart and wishes. Prayer, spending quality time with God is the key to a deeper more broken life.

Hearing and Obeying the Father's Wishes

As you develop this relationship with God as a child, you will begin to hear the secrets that only a Father tells his son or daughter.

What distinguishes a son from a servant? A servant only works for the master and gets paid for the work. You will rarely find the interaction between master and servant that brings forth intimacy of thought, heart, and mind.

Seldom does the relationship between the master and the servant increase to the levels of trust as it would with a son or daughter.

Now, to the son, the master is not a master! To the son, the master is his father. The tenderhearted concern, love, and purpose flow with a different rhythm. This is how our relationship will flow with the Father once we acknowledge our position of Sonship.

It's a Lifestyle!

Pleasing the Father is something we must do on a daily basis. It must be developed in us till it becomes automatic!

Pleasing the Father has nothing to do with church or ministry. It is totally a personal thing. It is the believer's chief principle and standard of living.

God will make sure to place the elements in our path, yes, elements that are conducive to this life I am talking about in this chapter.

God will do everything in His power to bring us to the place where we can learn this. Don't be shaken by the countless times God will challenge you to choose sides. It is all for the expansion of this one great and powerful truth, to please Him in all things, always. As

Jesus would say it, **"And He who sent Me is [always] with Me; He has not left Me alone, because I always do what pleases Him."** (John 8:29)

9

THE ELEMENT OF MINISTRY RELEASE
Why is the Thief the Treasurer?

"**But one of His disciples, Judas Iscariot, Simon's son, who would betray Him, said, 'Why was this fragrant oil not sold for three hundred denarii and given to the poor?' This he said, not that he cared for the poor, but because he was a thief, and had the money box, and he used to take what was put in it.**" (John 12:4-6)

I would like to turn your attention to this chapter and how often we find ourselves being tested by this element, the Element of Ministry Release.

When one of us is promoted to a position or entrusted with the responsibility to take over and oversee a project, the first thing a servant of the Lord needs to see is the why he or she is being entrusted with the position at hand. Why is the promotion coming your way?

Jesus Knew It All Along

Let's look at Jesus and His ministry here on earth. Here are some facts: Jesus chose the twelve disciples after spending a whole night in prayer. "**Now it came to pass in those days that He went out to the mountain to pray, and continued all night in prayer to God. And when it was day, He called His disciples to Him-**

self; and from them He chose twelve whom He also named apostles: Simon, whom He also named Peter, and Andrew his brother; James and John; Philip and Bartholomew; Matthew and Thomas; James the son of Alphaeus, and Simon called the Zealot; Judas the son of James, and Judas Iscariot who also became a traitor." (Luke 6:12-16)

By the text in Luke 6, we know that Jesus spent all night in prayer to God, and in the morning, He made His choice of whom would be His disciples.

There is a list there and it would be safe to say that God gave Jesus His son, this specific list of names.

In the names listed, there is an individual by the name of Judas Iscariot. Judas Iscariot didn't audition for this position; no, Judas Iscariot was literally chosen by the hand of God to be with Jesus and to learn about the kingdom of God.

Did Jesus know whom He was choosing? Did he know that these disciples were imperfect, rough around the edges, if you will? The answer is, yes, of course He did!

If Jesus knew that that these disciples were imperfect and needed a lot of work in their character, then why did He choose them? This is a legitimate question, so let us go deeper with it.

Why Was Judas Iscariot Chosen?

As imperfect in character as Judas Iscariot was, it is apparent that Jesus was only following the Father's wishes on this one. The Father probably told Jesus,

"Choose this guy. His name is Judas Iscariot. He is rough around the edges, but nevertheless, we will see his response to the grace and favor of God. If he chooses to walk in the kingdom, he will succeed; if he chooses to betray you, then he will disqualify himself." Fair enough!

As I ponder this story, I can't help but thinking of the many times God has chosen weak vessels to do His work. We all come to God as we are: imperfect, shameful, fearful, negative, weak, and to be honest, not qualified for anything. It is here that God's grace and favor is shown to us. What we do with this grace and favor, will determine our destiny.

Judas Iscariot obviously had some qualities and perhaps some gifts regarding the issue of money. He was probably good with numbers, and Jesus knew that. He pulled Judas aside and told him, "Judas, take care of the cash. I trust your judgement and your gifting. Here's the money box."

Somehow, someway, Judas found favor in the eyes of God and in the eyes of Jesus that he earned the position of treasurer.

He had the gift no doubt, but did he have the character required to save himself and others? There it is! The answer is no, he didn't have the character required!

Jesus knew that too, but he was willing to take a risk and develop this servant of God in character.

I believe that often God places us in positions that we are good at, only to educate us deeper and reveal to us, by way of loving judgment, our true nature.

We can't really change anything in us, until we

see ourselves as God truly sees us. It is at this place, that we will proceed to make the necessary changes that will align us with His character, the character of Christ.

God Will Test Us in our Gifting?

It might be that the Lord has been withholding a potential opportunity for advancement in your life due to some hidden character issue, and the Lord doesn't want you to hurt yourself severely.

He keeps you away from becoming a "superstar" a "mountain-mover," or "doesn't allow your healing, music, children, women's, prison ministry" to evolve the way you would like it to, why? Why would the Lord not permit you to flourish according to the stats, surveys, and opinions of others? Because the Father knows best!

So, for the Lord to reveal to you a ministry opportunity and for those over your life to acknowledge such a call on you and release you to where you can practice what God has instilled, is of utmost importance in the unfolding of destiny.

It is vital for God's servants to remember that if God has released you to a ministry opportunity— it will be a two-fold issue. First, you will be released to serve at a leadership capacity with all eyes of heaven being on you (not to mention your peers at church) and secondly, you will have an opportunity to keep your heart and mind and hands in check before God and man.

The time will come when the real you will come forth. The test will come and challenge you in every way possible. Your emotions, your decisions, your practical steps, how you deal with the applause and praise of man, and lastly, how you deal with the rejection of man. It will all come down to the decision of staying the course, looking for a shortcut, or in the case of Judas Iscariot, a desire for personal gain in betraying Jesus for thirty pieces of silver.

What the Value of Ministry Release Means

What this chapter really means is that you and I will be entrusted with an opportunity or perhaps more than one opportunity, to manifest our God-given gifts, talents, and abilities.

For those who walk with God and are ever conscious of God's character— opportunity will knock at your door. Someone will exalt you, trust you, applaud you, and even invest in you—what you do with that applause will be very telling of your own personal character.

God, who knows all things, will be watching your attitude, decision-making skills, your character development, more than your talents and abilities to handle a job, ministry, or vocation.

Just like He kept his eyes on Judas Iscariot when no other human being was paying attention to him; he saw Judas Iscariot hang out with the guys (disciples), He also saw Judas Iscariot hang out with the Roman soldiers, He also saw Judas Iscariot take some cash from the money box every time he could, and He finally saw Judas Iscariot's greed and opportunistic spirit get the best of him.

Teaching after teaching, miracle after miracle, Jesus was hoping for a better response from his then treasurer, but to no avail. Judas Iscariot perverted himself; he caught a glimpse of selfish greed and what it could bring to him, and the heart of Judas Iscariot deceived him into thinking that betraying Jesus was the highest honor in the sight of the Romans, and he bought into it.

As I close this chapter, my heart is broken, just thinking of how gracious God is with all of us and desires the best for all of us. Yet, our, "returning of the favor," sometimes does not compare with the sacrifice laid out on behalf of all of us sinners.

1 Corinthians 4:2 says, **"Moreover it is required in stewards that one be found faithful."** If we are to be God's vessels, then there are requirements. Be faithful with the opportunities allotted; do it with integrity, do it with fervency in your spirit, do it with passion in your soul, don't buy into the lies of the flesh, the devil, or the world.

Don't lose heart in the work of the Lord— Jesus said, **"Behold, I come quickly. My reward is with me, to repay to each man according to his work."** (Revelation 22:12 World English Bible)

10

THE ELEMENT OF DYING TO SELF
Was that Stephen's Last Message?

"And they chose Stephen, a man full of faith and the Holy Spirit..." (Acts 6:5b)

"And Stephen, full of faith and power, did great wonders and signs among the people." (Acts 6:8)

When I read of whom Stephen was and the works He did, I can't help but thinking that God has always been interested in using those who are willing to be used.

Now, the desire to be used by the Lord comes from deep within.

How does this happen? For starters, Stephen was a humble servant of the Lord and he was willing to do anything to advance the cause of Christ in the world.

His willingness and positive disposition to be used in any way possible make this man a candidate for greatness in God's army.

The Ministry of Stephen

The book of Acts gives us a bit of insight into who Stephen was and what type of man he was.

The need arose for widows to be taken care of, and since the apostles were busy in the word and prayer, they selected seven men to do the work of deacons [a fancy word for servants].

Well, Stephen was chosen as one of the seven and

so thus our story begins...

A Bright Future

When you think of this awesome humble servant Stephen, you can truly say, "This guy has a bright future in God's church!" "Stephen is going to be a great preacher and world-shaker for God one of these days!" or "Have you seen this unknown preacher? His name is Stephen! God is going to give him a big church or ministry one of these days, I just know it!"

All we can say is that Stephen had all the qualifications to be a great force in kingdom of God; his life was exemplary, not to mention, the power of God accompanied him with signs and wonder.

A Godly Opportunity

"Then there arose some from what is called the Synagogue of the Freedmen (Cyrenians, Alexandrians, and those from Cilicia and Asia), disputing with Stephen. And they were not able to resist the wisdom and the Spirit by which he spoke. Then they secretly induced men to say, 'We have heard him speak blasphemous words against Moses and God.' And they stirred up the people, the elders, and the scribes; and they came upon him, seized him, and brought him to the council. They also set up false witnesses who said, 'This man does not cease to speak blasphemous words against this holy place and the law; for we have heard him say that this Jesus of Nazareth will destroy this

place and change the customs which Moses delivered to us.' And all who sat in the council, looking steadfastly at him, saw his face as the face of an angel." (Acts 6:9-15)

It came to pass, during his calling as a deacon, that a situation arose—a disputing gang of religious people arose against Stephen. They raised false testimonies against Stephen, with the intent to get him in trouble, and perhaps even killed.

As the religious accused him to the high priest, the high priest said to Stephen, "Are these [accusations] so?"

From here, Stephen proceeded to preach one of the most powerful sermons ever recorded in history. Full of God and full of faith Stephen said, **"You stiff-necked and uncircumcised in heart and ears! You always resist the Holy Spirit; as your fathers did, so do you. Which of the prophets did your fathers not persecute? And they killed those who foretold the coming of the Just One, of whom you now have become the betrayers and murderers, who have received the law by the direction of angels and have not kept it."** (Acts 7:51-53)

As Stephen continued to press in with God's revelation, the religious group could not take it anymore and proceeded to attack him viciously and stoned him, just listen: **"When they heard these things they were cut to the heart, and they gnashed at him with their teeth. But he, being full of the Holy Spirit, gazed into heaven and saw the glory of God, and Jesus standing at the right hand of God, and said, 'Look! I see the heav-**

ens opened and the Son of Man standing at the right hand of God!' Then they cried out with a loud voice, stopped their ears, and ran at him with one accord; and they cast him out of the city and stoned him. And the witnesses laid down their clothes at the feet of a young man named Saul. And they stoned Stephen as he was calling on God and saying, 'Lord Jesus, receive my spirit.' Then he knelt down and cried out with a loud voice, 'Lord, do not charge them with this sin.' And when he had said this, he fell asleep."** (Acts 7:54-8:1)

Can you imagine this? Can you picture yourself just like Stephen, so bold and so fierce for Jesus' sake?

My question now is, what makes Stephen so outstanding amongst the brothers of his day? Why would Jesus open the heavens and allow Stephen to see this: **"Look! I see the heavens opened and the Son of Man standing at the right hand of God!"** Why would Jesus stand for Stephen?

Here's what I believe. I believe Jesus honors a man or woman who has died to self. I don't see Jesus standing for others like He did when Stephen (God's first martyr) was being stoned to death. Jesus Himself was ready to receive him with the highest honor. Blessed Lord Jesus.

It's protocol for citizens to pay homage to the king by kneeling and then standing before him in attention. Can you imagine the King of Kings doing this for you?

The Element of Dying to Self

God will allow things to come to us to prove our commitment, our faith, etc.

Once a man says to the Lord, "Here I am, send me," I believe God takes this to heart and begins a process to get us to the place where we need to be in God.

Stephen went all out in the name of Jesus! He didn't hold back; He didn't consider his life as valuable to himself. He saw everything in the light of eternity. This is what moves the heart of God.

Think about it: From seating at the right hand of God the Father (Colossians 3:1) to standing at the right hand of God (Acts 7:56)!

Now this is what I call a move of God!

Was that Stephen's Last Message?

One would naturally think and perhaps dare to say, "Stephen! Shut-Up! These guys are serious about killing you!" or "Stephen! You have a bright future. Don't mess it up. Just let them be!"

But no! Stephen was not going to stop because of fear! No Sir!

As people who are filled with the Spirit typically do, they prophesy to dry bones without fear and doubt! Stephen did just that.

He didn't consider his life, his future, or his family—no! All he could see was the spirit of religion keeping a whole generation in bondage...thus, he prophesied and spoke the Word of the Lord.

Maybe some might say, "So what was your point

Stephen, you got killed!" What was the result, Stephen? The result, in my own humble opinion, was that Saul of Tarsus was impacted by Stephen's words.

Challenged by a Nobody!

"Now Saul was consenting to his death. At that time a great persecution arose against the church that was at Jerusalem; and they were all scattered throughout the regions of Judea and Samaria, except the apostles. And devout men carried Stephen to his burial, and made great lamentation over him. As for Saul, he made havoc of the church, entering every house, and dragging off men and women, committing them to prison." (Acts 8:1-3)

I believe when Saul heard this young preacher prophesy under the power of God, and it shook "the daylights" out of him. Saul must have thought: "How dare this Stephen be more zealous than me!" And thus, the convicting power of God started to mess with Saul of Tarsus' life.

Could it be that God called out Stephen, a deacon, a man with no name, for the sake of breaking Saul of Tarsus?

I believe God had it all planned-out. Stephen breaks the outer shell of Saul of Tarsus and God catches up with Saul on the road to Damascus and meets him face to face for a powerful conversion. The rest is history!

Have you Died to Self?

Are you doing the works of God (by faith) or are you waiting for the right (pain-free) situation to come your way? To delay is to give oneself to fear and doubt. There is willful delay and there is God-led delay—which one are you under?

The element of dying to self will never change! God will forever test us on this one principle. If God needs work to be done and you have made yourself available unto Him by dying to self—then God will visit you and commission you.

11

THE ELEMENT OF PERSONAL BATTLES
Paul's Thorn and God's Sufficiency

"**And lest I should be exalted above measure by the abundance of the revelations, a thorn in the flesh was given to me, a messenger of Satan to buffet me, lest I be exalted above measure. Concerning this thing I pleaded with the Lord three times that it might depart from me. And He said to me, 'My grace is sufficient for you, for My strength is made perfect in weakness.' Therefore most gladly I will rather boast in my infirmities, that the power of Christ may rest upon me. Therefore I take pleasure in infirmities, in reproaches, in needs, in persecutions, in distresses, for Christ's sake. For when I am weak, then I am strong.'"** (2 Corinthians 12:7-10)

According to Paul's testimony and all he saw in the spirit— he felt that God had allowed a **"thorn in the flesh"** to buffet him. In other words, due to the temptation of becoming something great in the eyes of man, God allowed some personal struggle to keep Paul in check— something that would keep him humble. I don't claim to understand it all, but something happened to Paul after God allowed this "thorn in the flesh" to have its way in his life.

The Making of a Vessel of God

The making of a vessel is not an easy thing. Those who say, "Yes!" to the Lord, will live in a very different world.

For starters, the guard that God keeps on his vessel is very distinct. He will not allow his vessel to be exalted above measure, but will do anything to keep him in a place where he won't stumble over worldly things.

Whatever it is that we need in our own personal life that will keep us seeking, hungry, humble and broken – God will allow!

I know that sometimes it can be difficult understanding the sovereignty of God at work in us.

As the Lord does His deep work in us, we tend to use our theology of what we know of God to veer off the "test," "the enemy," etc.

It is not until we understand our "trial" from God's perspective that the element of personal struggle is understood.

The Lord will not allow anything that is not of His Spirit to invade our lives and cause us to be detoured from His eternal plan for us. He is a Jealous God!

Lusting After Externals

In my experience of walking with Jesus, I have tasted and seen the awesomeness of God's presence. I have been touched by Him and commissioned to follow hard after Him.

But to be fair and balanced, I have also felt the horrific temptation of forsaking God's commission for my life, the very task God has given me; and exchange that glory for worldly comfort and earthly glory and recognition.

Often, I have tried to justify my carnal longings. I have made every attempt to convince myself that it's ok to have a little of this or a little of that—and like a refinery's fire burning within me, I hear His words screaming in my soul, **"Man shall not live by bread alone, but by every word that proceeds from the mouth of God!"**

So, in the same way, it is for God that we have been saved, called and commissioned for His purposes alone.

For some reason the words of Paul come to mind, **"...and He died for all, that those who live should live no longer for themselves, but for Him who died for them and rose again."** (2 Corinthians 5:15)

The Real Battle Is . . .

The real battle that you and I have as we walk in God's kingdom is the temptation to be "somebody." The continual inward desire for significance, acceptance, and adoption from some other source apart from God's work in us, is a wicked lie.

It is the devil's duty to make us look elsewhere for significance, acceptance, and adoption. My friends, Jesus is Enough!

If Anyone Deserved Recognition, It Would Be . . .

I have found that if there were any believer during

the primitive years of the church who had any or deserved any fame, it would have been Paul.

No one that we know of (during the days of Paul) had experienced God in such a magnitude as he did. He was a firebrand for Jesus and yet God would not let him get away with all this glory.

If Paul would have wanted— he could have built the first megachurch of his day. He could have had the greatest conferences and seminars of his day. Can you imagine Paul's name being paraded on flyers and colorful brochures all over Asia Minor: FIRE CONFERENCE with the one and only Apostle Paul, *"Come and receive your miracle!"* Or *"Come for a time of exciting revelation and prophetic insight!"* Can you really see Paul caught up in the same game that we all get caught up in? I can't see that for the life of me! Not in the Apostle Paul's ministry.

Your Personal Struggle Is God's Workshop for You!

As we long to know God, we will discover that God's treatment of us is really a special one. He won't allow you to go through life like other believers do.

Your visions and revelations from the Lord are unique, but so are your personal struggles.

You might be tempted to complain to the Lord, but you need to realize, or at least keep in mind that this is the way that God has specifically chosen, to do it with you! We must rest in that.

In the element of personal struggles, you and I will discover that there will be many of these in our lifetime. All our personal struggles have a specific significance and assignment.

Though God shows us great revelations and brings to us great ministry opportunities; know that struggles may also present themselves in mighty ways.

"My Strength Made Perfect in Weakness."

As I close this chapter, I want you to know that if God called you to walk with Him, He will see you through and through. No matter what comes against you—God is able to sustain you—for when you are weak, God is strong!

God has promised to keep you until the end. Listen to these Scriptures:

"The LORD is your keeper; The LORD is your shade on your right hand." (Psalms 121:5)

"For I am confident of this very thing, that He who began a good work in you will perfect it until the day of Christ Jesus." (Philippians 1:6)

12

THE ELEMENT OF FIERY FURNACES
"Did we not cast three men bound into the midst of the fire?"

"Therefore at that time certain Chaldeans came forward and accused the Jews. They spoke and said to King Nebuchadnezzar, 'O king, live forever! You, O king, have made a decree that everyone who hears the sound of the horn, flute, harp, lyre, and psaltery, in symphony with all kinds of music, shall fall down and worship the gold image; and whoever does not fall down and worship shall be cast into the midst of a burning fiery furnace. There are certain Jews whom you have set over the affairs of the province of Babylon: Shadrach, Meshach, and Abed-Nego; these men, O king, have not paid due regard to you. They do not serve your gods or worship the gold image which you have set up.'" (Daniel 3:8-12)

"Then King Nebuchadnezzar was astonished; and he rose in haste and spoke, saying to his counselors, 'Did we not cast three men bound into the midst of the fire?' They answered and said to the king, 'True, O king.' 'Look!' he answered, 'I see four men loose, walking in the midst of the fire; and they are not hurt, and the form of the fourth is like the Son of God.'" (Daniel 3:24-25)

I want to turn your attention now to the element

of fire and how the fiery furnaces in our lives play a huge roll in our personal and spiritual development.

It is one thing to be a "Christian" by religion status and totally different thing to be a Vessel of God and for God.

You might ask, "Well, what is the big difference?" The big difference is found in the attitude you take when you discover all that God has intended for your life now that you have been converted and now experiencing kingdom life.

A Vessel of Honor

"But in a great house there are not only vessels of gold and silver, but also of wood and clay, some for honor and some for dishonor. Therefore if anyone cleanses himself from the latter, he will be a vessel for honor, sanctified and useful for the Master, prepared for every good work." (2 Timothy 2:20-21)

Let me start by saying that Paul simplified it for us in this one verse. He said that in a house there are all kinds of vessels. Some are made of gold and silver, while others are made of wood and clay. Their uses also vary. Some are used for honorable things, while others are used for not so honorable things.

Whether you understand what kind of use the Master has in mind or not, the point of cleansing the vessel before its use is vital to your development.

While we make the attempt to understand why some of our "trials" are different than someone else's, we must also keep in mind that the Master has also revealed the use for this vessel or that one.

Depending on the use of the vessel, the degree of intense fire is set. The degree of usefulness will determine the degree of intensity in the fiery furnace.

Before we start falling into despair and discouragement, it would be wise for us to get a glimpse of what kind of vessel God has set us to be. This will define much of why this element is so vital to us.

Enlargement Is Coming!

One of the things I have learned about the fiery furnace is this: it has its own culture and its own way of breaking anyone who comes into it.

One can boast about his or her life; one can talk about all their accomplishments in the faith, business and ministry, while others speak of their prosperity.

My friends, all these have one thing in common: the lack of fire, holy fire!

The element of fiery furnaces has a special way of "squeezing the honey" out of us. When this holy burning starts doing its thing, the first thing to dissipate is our flesh. The flesh can't stand the presence of God!

The burning starts to consume all the flesh: our own means for survival, our ideas, our philosophies, our theologies, our preconceived notions, potions, and emotions. It burns like the chaff!

Meshach, Shadrach and Abednego were taken into a fiery furnace, and boy was it hot! The soldiers (who by the way were mighty men of valor) who put them in the furnace died due to the intense heat. The hotter the furnace became, the greater the potential for a great testimony.

The Scripture goes on to say that King Nebuchadnezzar was astonished when he saw the fire burning and the three men were not burned; and not only that, but he inquired that if it wasn't only three men they had originally put inside, then who is that fourth men walking in the furnace with the other three? His form is that of the Son of God!

Christ appeared right in the middle of the fiery furnace. This is the pattern for those who begin to trust the element of the fiery furnace.

The only way to know God is through the revelation of His appearing in the middle of our fiery furnace. I know "Christians" in general, know very little about this type of walk and even less of the development of a vessel.

Once the fiery furnace kicks-in into full throttle, there are several things that will come forth from it, let me share them with you:

Fire will enlarge our capacity for God. When we enter His furnace, our desire to know God increases. Our capacity to go deeper with God increases. We become more and more preoccupied with having more of God within us. As the test continues, an enlargement is taking place, whether we know it or not.

Fire will enlarge our vision for God. Fire has a way of consuming our selfish desires. Limited-thinking people are very selfish people. They only think of what they can do, but never consider what God can do—of course, if they would only "let go," they would see. As we are being placed in a fiery furnace of testing, God will enlarge our vision for God; after much testing, God will appear bigger than what we originally thought!

Fire will enlarge our borders for God. It's amazing what one can learn by allowing God to teach him or her a thing or two. Our minds tend to follow patterns and structured thinking. When God's fire is set upon our lives, those patterns burn off—our borders widen and the possibilities begin to appear.

Fire will enlarge our ministries for God. Lastly, once the fire of God's fiery furnace accomplishes its purpose, our ministry opportunities will be enlarged. We will not have to try hard to prove our ministry worth to anyone for the Lord Himself will open countless doors so that we (tested and approved vessels) can glorify His Name in other lands, countries, churches, businesses, etc.

There is not a more powerful cleansing agent than His purifying fire! Listen to Malachi: **"BEHOLD, I send My messenger, and he shall prepare the way before Me. And the Lord [the Messiah], Whom you seek, will suddenly come to His temple; the Messenger or Angel of the covenant, Whom you desire, behold, He shall come, says the Lord of hosts.** [Matt. 11:10; Luke 1:13-17, 76.] **But who can endure the day of His coming? And who can stand when He appears? For He is like a refiner's fire and like fullers' soap.** [Rev. 6:12-17.] **He will sit as a refiner and purifier of silver, and He will purify the priests, the sons of Levi, and refine them like gold and silver, that they may offer to the Lord offerings in righteousness."** (Malachi 3:1-3 - Amplified Bible)

Ministry Resources

THE FEW
The Call to the Road Less Traveled-
The Call to Intimacy with God.
ISBN-9780999171004

LOS POCOS
Un LLamado al Camino Menos Transitado
- El Llamado a la Intimidad Con Dios
ISBN-9780999171028

THE HEART OF DAVID JOURNAL - *VOLUME 1*
(Hardback)
ISBN-9780999171035

All Books Can Be Purchased at
www.shabarpublications.com

Ministry Information

For more information regarding the ministry of Masterbuilder Ministries, Inc., preaching engagements, leadership training seminars, etc. feel free to email Pastor David Mayorga at mayorga1126@gmail.com.

Check-Out our Websites:

    www.masterbuildertx.com

    www.shabarpublications.com

    www.dmayorga.com

www.ingramcontent.com/pod-product-compliance
Lightning Source LLC
Chambersburg PA
CBHW050544300426
44113CB00012B/2255